WILLS UNVEILED: A COMPREHENSIVE GUIDE TO UNDERSTANDING WILLS FOR EVERYDAY INDIVIDUALS

I. Introduction

A. Importance of Wills

Wills play a crucial role in estate planning and ensuring that your wishes are carried out after your passing. Here are some key reasons highlighting the importance of having a will:

1. Distribution of Assets: A will allows you to specify how your assets, such as property, investments, and personal belongings, should be distributed among your loved ones. Without a will, the distribution may be subject to intestacy laws, which might not align with your desires.

2. Guardianship of Minor Children: If you have children who are minors, a will enables you to appoint a guardian of your choice. This ensures that someone you trust will take care of your children and make important decisions on their behalf.

3. Avoiding Family Conflicts: Having a clear and legally binding will can help minimize potential disputes among family members. It provides a transparent framework for asset distribution, reducing the likelihood of disagreements or legal battles after your passing.

4. Protecting Unmarried Partners: For unmarried couples, a will is essential to ensure that your partner receives assets and inheritances according to your wishes. Without a will, unmarried partners may not be recognized under intestacy laws, potentially leaving them without any legal entitlement.

5. Minimizing Estate Taxes: A well-structured will can help minimize the tax burden on your estate. By utilizing tax planning strategies, you can potentially reduce the amount of estate taxes that your beneficiaries may have to pay.

6. Naming an Executor: In your will, you can appoint an executor who will be responsible for managing your estate, paying debts, and distributing assets. This allows you to choose someone you trust and who is capable of handling these important responsibilities.

7. Peace of Mind: Creating a will provides peace of mind by ensuring that your final wishes are known and documented. It allows you to have control over your legacy and provides reassurance that your loved ones will be taken care of according to your intentions.

It is important to consult with a legal professional or estate planning attorney to ensure that your will is properly drafted and legally enforceable. They can provide guidance tailored to your specific circumstances and help you navigate the complexities of estate planning.

B. Common Myths and Misconceptions

There are several common myths and misconceptions surrounding wills and estate planning. Let's address a few of them:

1. "I don't need a will because I don't have many assets."
   - Regardless of the size of your estate, having a will is important. It ensures that your assets are distributed according to your wishes and can help avoid legal complications or disputes.

2. "I'm too young to create a will."
   - It's never too early to create a will. Life is unpredictable, and having a will in place ensures that your wishes are known even if something unexpected happens. It's especially important if you have dependents or specific desires for asset distribution.

3. "Creating a will is expensive and complicated."
   - While it's true that consulting with an attorney can be helpful, creating a basic will can be relatively straightforward and affordable. There are also online resources and software that can assist in creating a simple will. However, for more complex situations, professional guidance is recommended.

4. "Once I create a will, I can never change it."

- Wills are not set in stone. You can update and modify your will as your circumstances change. Major life events such as marriage, divorce, birth of children, or changes in assets may require adjustments to your will.

5. "A will covers all my assets."
    - A will covers assets that are solely in your name. It may not cover assets that have designated beneficiaries or assets held in joint tenancy or trusts. It's important to review and align beneficiary designations and ownership arrangements with your will.

6. "Probate is always a lengthy and expensive process."
    - While probate can be time-consuming and involve legal fees, it's not always an onerous process. The complexity and duration of probate can vary depending on the size of the estate, state laws, and any potential disputes. Proper estate planning can help minimize probate complications.

7. "I can rely on verbal promises or informal agreements."
    - Verbal promises or informal agreements may not hold up legally after your passing. Having a written will ensures that your wishes are clearly documented and legally enforceable.

Remember, it's essential to consult with legal professionals or estate planning attorneys to address your specific needs and ensure that your will is valid and effective. They can provide personalized guidance and help dispel any further myths or misconceptions you may have.

II. What is a Will?

A. Definition and Purpose

A will is a legal document that outlines a person's wishes regarding the distribution of their assets and the management of their affairs after their death. It is commonly used in estate planning to ensure that an individual's desires are carried out and their assets are distributed according to their wishes.

The primary purpose of a will is to provide instructions on how to distribute property, assets, and possessions after death. This includes specifying who will inherit the assets, such as family members, friends, or charitable organizations. A will can also designate guardians for minor children and outline any specific funeral or burial wishes.

In addition to asset distribution, a will can serve other important purposes, such as:

1. Appointing an executor: A will allows you to name an executor, who is responsible for managing the estate, paying debts, and distributing assets according to the instructions in the will.

2. Minimizing family disputes: By clearly stating your wishes in a legally binding document, a will can help prevent potential conflicts and disputes among family members regarding asset distribution.

3. Protecting minor children: A will can designate a guardian for minor children, ensuring that their care and well-being are provided for in the event of your death.

4. Expressing charitable intentions: If you have philanthropic goals or specific charities you wish to support, a will allows you to include provisions for charitable donations.

5. Avoiding intestacy laws: Without a valid will, your assets may be distributed according to intestacy laws, which may not align with your wishes. Creating a will ensures that you have control over how your assets are distributed.

Overall, a will provides peace of mind by allowing individuals to have a say in what happens to their assets and affairs after their passing. It is an essential tool in estate planning and can help ensure that your loved ones are taken care of and your wishes are respected.

    B.   **Key Components of a Will**

A will typically consists of several key components that are essential for it to be legally valid and effective. These components include:

1. Personal Information: A will begins with your personal information, including your full name, address, and date of birth. This helps identify you as the creator of the will.

2. Executor: The will designates an executor, also known as a personal representative or executor, who is responsible for carrying out the instructions outlined in the will. This person is typically a trusted individual or a professional executor.

3. Asset Inventory: A comprehensive list of your assets should be included in the will. This can include real estate, bank accounts, investments, vehicles, personal belongings, and any other valuable possessions.

4. Beneficiaries: The will specifies who will inherit your assets after your death. Beneficiaries can include family members, friends, charities, or other organizations. It is important to clearly identify each beneficiary and the specific assets they will receive.

5. Guardianship: If you have minor children, a will allows you to designate a guardian who will take care of them in the event of your death. This is a crucial component for ensuring the well-being and custody of your children.

6. Distribution of Assets: The will outlines how your assets will be distributed among your beneficiaries. This can be done by specifying percentages, specific items, or a combination of both. You can also include any conditions or restrictions for the distribution of assets.

7. Alternate Beneficiaries: It is advisable to include alternate beneficiaries in case the primary beneficiaries predecease you or are unable to inherit the assets for any reason. This ensures that your assets are distributed according to your wishes.

8. Residual Clause: A residual clause addresses any assets or property that are not specifically mentioned in the will. It states how these remaining assets should be distributed.

9. Witnesses and Signatures: To make the will legally valid, it must be signed by you, the creator of the will, in the presence of witnesses. The number of witnesses required varies by jurisdiction, but it is typically two or more. The witnesses must also sign the will.

It is important to consult with a legal professional or estate planning attorney when creating a will to ensure that all the necessary components are included and that it complies with the laws and requirements of your jurisdiction.

III. Why Do You Need a Will?

A. Ensuring Your Wishes are Followed

Ensuring that your wishes are followed after your passing involves taking certain steps and considerations. Here are some ways to help ensure that your wishes are followed:

1. Create a Will: Creating a legally valid will is crucial for outlining your wishes regarding the distribution of your assets, appointing an executor, and specifying guardianship for minor children. Work with an estate planning attorney to draft a clear and comprehensive will that reflects your intentions.

2. Review and Update Your Will: Regularly review and update your will to reflect any changes in your circumstances, such as the birth of children, marriage, divorce, or changes in your assets. Keep your will up to date to ensure that it accurately represents your wishes.

3. Communicate Your Wishes: It is important to communicate your wishes to your loved ones and those involved in executing your will. This can help prevent misunderstandings and ensure that everyone is aware of your intentions.

4. Choose a Trusted Executor: Select an executor who is trustworthy, capable, and willing to carry out your wishes. Discuss your expectations with the chosen executor and make sure they are aware of their responsibilities.

5. Consider a Trust: Depending on your circumstances and goals, setting up a trust can provide additional control and flexibility in managing your assets and ensuring they are distributed according to your wishes. Trusts can also help avoid probate and provide privacy.

6. Keep Important Documents Secure: Store your will and other important documents, such as insurance policies, bank account information, and property deeds, in a secure location. Inform your loved ones of the location and provide them with access instructions.

7. Communicate with Professionals: Regularly consult with professionals such as your attorney, financial advisor, and accountant to ensure that your assets and financial affairs are properly managed and aligned with your wishes.

8. Review Beneficiary Designations: Regularly review and update beneficiary designations for your retirement accounts, life insurance policies, and other assets that pass outside of your will. Make sure these designations reflect your current wishes.

9. Consider Advance Directives: In addition to a will, consider creating advance directives such as a living will and healthcare power of attorney. These documents outline your healthcare preferences and appoint someone to make medical decisions on your behalf if you become incapacitated.

10. Seek Professional Advice: It is highly recommended to seek professional advice from an estate planning attorney to ensure that your wishes are legally protected and properly documented. They can help you navigate the complexities of estate planning and provide guidance based on your specific circumstances.

Remember, it is crucial to consult with a legal professional to ensure that your estate planning documents comply with the laws and requirements of your jurisdiction.

B. Protecting Your Loved Ones

Protecting your loved ones involves taking steps to ensure their well-being and financial security. Here are some ways to protect your loved ones:

1. Life Insurance: Consider purchasing life insurance to provide financial support to your loved ones in the event of your untimely passing. Life insurance can help cover expenses such as funeral costs, outstanding debts, and provide income replacement for your family.

2. Health Insurance: Ensure that you and your loved ones have adequate health insurance coverage. This will help protect against unexpected medical expenses and ensure access to necessary healthcare services.

3. Estate Planning: Create a comprehensive estate plan that includes a will, trust, and other necessary documents. This will help ensure that your assets are distributed according to your wishes and provide for the financial needs of your loved ones.

4. Appoint a Guardian: If you have minor children, designate a guardian who will take care of them in the event of your passing. Choose someone who is capable and willing to assume this responsibility and discuss your wishes with them.

5. Power of Attorney: Consider granting a power of attorney to a trusted individual who can make financial and legal decisions on your behalf if you become incapacitated. This will ensure that your affairs are managed properly and your loved ones' needs are taken care of.

6. Designate Beneficiaries: Review and update beneficiary designations on your retirement accounts, life insurance policies, and other assets. Designating beneficiaries ensures that these assets pass directly to your chosen individuals without going through the probate process.

7. Communicate Your Wishes: Clearly communicate your wishes to your loved ones and ensure that they have access to important documents such as your will, insurance policies, and financial accounts. This will help them understand your intentions and facilitate the implementation of your plans.

8. Emergency Fund: Build an emergency fund to provide a financial safety net for your loved ones. Having savings in place can help cover unexpected expenses and provide stability during difficult times.

9. Education Planning: If you have children, consider setting up education savings accounts or trusts to help fund their education expenses. Planning for their future education shows your commitment to their long-term well-being.

10. Seek Professional Advice: Consult with financial advisors, estate planning attorneys, and insurance professionals to ensure that you have the right strategies in place to protect your loved ones. They can provide personalized guidance based on your specific needs and goals.

Remember, protecting your loved ones requires ongoing review and adjustments as your circumstances change. Regularly revisit your plans to ensure they align with your current situation and priorities.

C. Distributing Your Assets

Distributing your assets involves the process of dividing your property and belongings among your beneficiaries after your passing. Here are some steps to consider when distributing your assets:

1. Create a Will: Draft a legally binding will that clearly states your wishes regarding the distribution of your assets. Specify who will receive what, and consider naming an executor to oversee the distribution process.

2. Seek Legal Advice: Consult with an experienced estate planning attorney to ensure that your will is properly prepared and meets all

legal requirements. They can guide you through the process and help you address any complex issues that may arise.

3. Consider Trusts: Explore the option of setting up trusts to distribute your assets. Trusts can provide additional control and flexibility in asset distribution, especially for individuals with significant assets or specific concerns, such as providing for minor children or individuals with special needs.

4. Review Beneficiary Designations: Regularly review and update beneficiary designations on your financial accounts, retirement plans, life insurance policies, and other assets. Ensure that your chosen beneficiaries are up to date and reflect your current wishes.

5. Consider Tax Implications: Take into account any potential tax implications when distributing your assets. Certain assets may have tax consequences for your beneficiaries, and it is important to understand and plan for these potential liabilities.

6. Communicate Your Intentions: Clearly communicate your intentions to your loved ones and the executor of your will. Provide them with copies of your will and any other relevant documents, and discuss your wishes openly to minimize potential disputes and confusion.

7. Keep Records: Keep detailed records of your assets, debts, and any instructions regarding their distribution. This will make it easier for your executor to locate and manage your assets after your passing.

8. Regularly Update Your Plan: Review and update your estate plan periodically or whenever significant life events occur, such as marriage, divorce, the birth of children, or the acquisition of new assets. This ensures that your plan remains current and reflects your changing circumstances and wishes.

9. Consider Charitable Giving: If you wish to leave a portion of your assets to charitable organizations, include these provisions in your estate plan. Consult with an attorney or financial advisor to explore

the most effective ways to incorporate charitable giving into your distribution strategy.

10. Involve Professionals: Work with professionals such as estate planning attorneys and financial advisors to ensure that your assets are distributed according to your wishes and in the most efficient manner possible. They can help navigate complex legal and financial matters and provide guidance throughout the process.

Remember, distributing your assets is a highly individualized process, and it's important to consult with professionals who can provide personalized advice based on your specific circumstances and goals.

IV. Types of Wills

A. Simple Wills

A simple will is a legal document that outlines how you want your assets and property to be distributed after your passing. While the complexity of a will can vary depending on individual circumstances, a simple will typically includes the following key elements:

1. Personal Information: Start by stating your full name, address, and other relevant personal details.

2. Appointment of Executor: Designate an executor, also known as a personal representative, who will be responsible for carrying out the instructions in your will. Choose someone you trust and discuss their willingness to take on this role before making the appointment.

3. Beneficiaries: Clearly identify who you want to inherit your assets. This can include family members, friends, or charitable

organizations. You can specify what percentage or specific assets each beneficiary will receive.

4. Guardianship: If you have minor children, specify who you want to be their legal guardian. This is especially important if the other parent is not alive or able to fulfill this role.

5. Specific Gifts: You may choose to leave specific items or assets to specific individuals. These can include sentimental items, family heirlooms, or other personal belongings.

6. Residual Estate: Specify how you want the remainder of your estate to be distributed after all debts, taxes, and specific gifts have been accounted for. This can be divided equally among beneficiaries or according to your specific wishes.

7. Alternate Beneficiaries: In case a beneficiary predeceases you or is unable to inherit for any reason, name alternate beneficiaries who will receive the assets instead.

8. Funeral and Burial Wishes: Although not legally binding, you can include your preferences for your funeral arrangements and burial or cremation.

9. Witnesses and Signatures: Most jurisdictions require wills to be witnessed by two or more individuals who are not beneficiaries or closely related to beneficiaries. Ensure that all necessary signatures are included to make the will valid.

It's important to consult with an estate planning attorney to ensure that your simple will is properly executed and complies with the laws of your jurisdiction. They can provide guidance based on your specific circumstances and help you create a legally binding document that reflects your wishes.

B. Living Wills

A living will, also known as an advance healthcare directive, is a legal document that outlines your preferences for medical treatment in the event that you become unable to communicate or make decisions for yourself. It allows you to express your wishes regarding medical care and end-of-life decisions, ensuring that your healthcare providers and loved ones know how to proceed.

Here are some key points to consider when creating a living will:

1. Medical Treatments: Specify the medical treatments or interventions you would like to receive or refuse. This can include decisions about resuscitation, life-sustaining measures, pain management, and organ donation.

2. End-of-Life Care: Outline your preferences for end-of-life care, such as whether you would like to be kept comfortable with pain medication, receive hospice care, or be placed on life support if your condition is irreversible.

3. Quality of Life: Describe what quality of life means to you and indicate under what circumstances you would not want certain treatments to be administered if they would only prolong your suffering without a reasonable chance of recovery.

4. Healthcare Proxy: Consider appointing a healthcare proxy, also known as a durable power of attorney for healthcare. This is a person you trust to make medical decisions on your behalf if you are unable to do so. Discuss your wishes with your chosen healthcare proxy to ensure they understand and are willing to fulfill this role.

5. Legal Requirements: Familiarize yourself with the legal requirements of your jurisdiction regarding living wills. Some jurisdictions may require specific language or the presence of witnesses or a notary for the document to be valid.

It's important to discuss your living will with your healthcare provider, loved ones, and the person you have appointed as your healthcare proxy. Make sure they understand your wishes and have copies of the living will readily accessible. Keep in mind that a living will can be revised or updated as your circumstances or preferences change, so it's a good idea to review and update it periodically.

Consulting with an attorney or legal professional experienced in estate planning and healthcare directives can help ensure that your living will accurately reflects your wishes and is legally valid in your jurisdiction.

C. Joint Wills

A joint will is a legal document created by a couple that combines both partners' wishes for the distribution of their assets and property after their deaths. Unlike individual wills, which are separate documents for each person, a joint will is a single document that represents the mutual agreement and intentions of both partners.

Here are some key points to understand about joint wills:

1. Shared Wishes: A joint will allows a couple to express their shared wishes for the distribution of their assets. It typically includes provisions for the transfer of property, naming of beneficiaries, and any specific instructions or conditions.

2. Simplicity and Convenience: By creating a joint will, a couple can simplify the estate planning process, as they only need to maintain and update a single document. This can be convenient for couples who have similar or identical wishes for the distribution of their assets.

3. Limitations: It's important to note that joint wills can limit the flexibility of each individual in making changes to their portion of the will. Once one partner passes away, the surviving partner is bound by the terms of the joint will and may not be able to make changes independently.

4. Survivorship Clause: Joint wills often include a survivorship clause, which outlines what should happen to the remaining assets when the first partner passes away. This clause typically states that the entire estate will be transferred to the surviving partner, and the distribution will occur only after the death of the surviving partner.

5. Considerations: While joint wills can be convenient, they may not be suitable for all couples. It's important to consider factors such as the complexity of your assets, potential changes in circumstances, and the desire for individual control over your own will.

Consulting with an attorney or legal professional who specializes in estate planning is crucial when considering joint wills. They can provide guidance on the legal implications, potential drawbacks, and alternatives that may better suit your specific needs and circumstances.

Remember, estate planning is a personal and complex matter, and it's important to carefully consider your options and seek professional advice to ensure that your wishes are properly documented and legally valid.

D. Holographic Wills

A holographic will, also known as a handwritten will, is a legal document that is entirely handwritten and signed by the testator (the person creating the will). Unlike a typed or printed will, a holographic will does not require witnesses to be legally valid in some jurisdictions.

Here are some key points to understand about holographic wills:

1. Handwritten and Signed: A holographic will must be entirely handwritten by the testator. It should include all the necessary provisions, such as the distribution of assets, appointment of executors, and guardianship for minor children. The will must also be signed by the testator.

2. No Witnesses Required: In some jurisdictions, holographic wills do not require witnesses. This means that the will can be created and signed by the testator without any other individuals present. However, it's important to note that some jurisdictions may have specific requirements regarding witnesses, so it's advisable to consult local laws or seek legal advice.

3. Informal Nature: Holographic wills are often considered informal compared to traditional wills. They may not follow a specific format or include legal jargon. However, it's important to ensure that the intentions and provisions are clear and unambiguous to avoid any potential disputes or challenges.

4. Limited to Handwriting: Holographic wills must be entirely handwritten by the testator. This means that any typed, printed, or pre-printed sections may invalidate the will. Additionally, any amendments or changes to the holographic will must also be handwritten and signed by the testator.

5. Validity and Challenges: The validity of holographic wills can vary depending on the jurisdiction. Some jurisdictions recognize holographic wills as legally binding, while others may require witnesses or additional formalities. It's important to understand the laws in your specific jurisdiction to ensure the validity of a holographic will.

6. Considerations: While holographic wills can be convenient, they may also pose challenges. Handwritten wills may be more prone to misunderstandings, misinterpretations, or disputes. Additionally, the absence of witnesses can make it difficult to prove the authenticity of the will.

It's important to note that holographic wills may not be suitable for everyone. Consulting with an attorney or legal professional who specializes in estate planning can provide guidance on the legal requirements, potential drawbacks, and alternative options that may better suit your specific needs and circumstances.

Remember, estate planning is a crucial aspect of protecting your assets and ensuring your wishes are carried out. It's important to carefully consider your options, seek professional advice, and ensure that your will is properly executed and legally valid.

V. Creating Your Will

A. Choosing an Executor

Choosing an executor for your estate is an important decision when creating a will or estate plan. The executor, also known as a personal representative or executor of the will, is responsible for carrying out your wishes as outlined in your will and managing the administration of your estate. Here are some considerations to keep in mind when choosing an executor:

1. Trustworthiness and Integrity: Select someone you trust to act in your best interests and carry out your wishes faithfully. The executor should be someone with integrity, honesty, and a sense of responsibility.

2. Organizational and Administrative Skills: The executor will be responsible for managing various tasks, such as locating and valuing assets, paying debts and taxes, distributing assets to beneficiaries, and handling legal and financial paperwork. Choose someone who is organized, detail-oriented, and capable of handling administrative duties effectively.

3. Availability and Time Commitment: Being an executor can be time-consuming, especially during the estate administration process. Consider someone who has the time and availability to fulfill the duties required. Executors should be willing and able to dedicate the necessary time and effort to carry out their responsibilities.

4. Financial Responsibility: The executor may need to handle financial matters, such as managing bank accounts, paying bills, and filing taxes. It is beneficial to choose someone who is financially responsible and has a good understanding of financial matters or is willing to seek professional advice if needed.

5. Knowledge of the Law: While not mandatory, it can be helpful if the executor has some knowledge of estate laws and regulations. If your estate is complex or involves unique circumstances, it may be advisable to select an executor who has experience in estate planning or is willing to work closely with an attorney.

6. Age and Health: Consider the age and health of the potential executor. It is important to choose someone who is likely to outlive you and is in good health. This ensures that they will be able to carry out their duties when the time comes.

7. Willingness to Serve: Before appointing someone as an executor, have a conversation with them to ensure they are willing to take on the role. Being an executor requires time, effort, and responsibility, so it is essential to choose someone who is willing to fulfill this role.

8. Multiple Executors or Professionals: You can choose to have multiple executors or even appoint a professional executor, such as a lawyer or trust company. This may be appropriate if your estate is complex, if there is potential for conflicts among beneficiaries, or if you want to ensure impartiality and expertise in the administration process.

Ultimately, the choice of executor should be based on your individual circumstances and the specific requirements of your estate. It is important to discuss your decision with the potential executor and seek their consent before finalizing your choice. Additionally, consulting with an attorney or estate planning professional can provide valuable guidance and ensure that your choice of executor aligns with your overall estate planning goals.

B. Identifying Beneficiaries

Identifying beneficiaries is a crucial step in estate planning. Beneficiaries are the individuals or entities who will receive your assets or property after your passing. Here are some considerations to help you identify beneficiaries:

1. Immediate Family: Start by considering your immediate family members, such as your spouse, children, or grandchildren. They are often the first choice for many people when it comes to beneficiaries.

2. Extended Family: Think about other family members, such as siblings, parents, nieces, nephews, or cousins, who you may want to include as beneficiaries. Consider the relationships you have with them and whether you want to leave them a portion of your assets.

3. Close Friends: You may have close friends who are like family to you. If you wish to include them as beneficiaries, consider their importance in your life and the impact you would like to have on their future.

4. Charitable Organizations: If you have a cause or charity that is close to your heart, you may choose to name them as beneficiaries. This allows you to leave a lasting impact and support a cause that aligns with your values.

5. Business Partners or Employees: If you own a business, you may consider including your business partners or key employees as beneficiaries. This can ensure the continuity of the business and provide for those who have contributed to its success.

6. Trusts or Foundations: You may choose to establish a trust or foundation and name it as a beneficiary. This allows you to provide ongoing support to specific causes or individuals over an extended period.

7. Special Circumstances: Consider any special circumstances or unique situations that may require special consideration. For example, if you have a dependent with special needs, you may need to set up a trust to ensure their long-term care and financial support.

When identifying beneficiaries, it is essential to communicate your intentions clearly and openly with those involved. Discuss your plans with your loved ones and ensure that they understand your wishes. Additionally, consult with an attorney or estate planning professional to help you navigate the legal requirements and ensure that your beneficiary designations are properly documented.

Keep in mind that estate planning is a personal and individualized process. The choice of beneficiaries should reflect your values, priorities, and desires for the distribution of your assets. Regularly review your beneficiary designations to ensure they align with your current circumstances and make any necessary updates as life events occur.

C. Listing Your Assets and Debts

Listing your assets and debts is an important step in managing your finances and planning for the future. Here are some guidelines to help you create a comprehensive list:

1. Assets:
   - Real Estate: Include any properties you own, such as your primary residence, vacation homes, rental properties, or land.
   - Financial Accounts: List all your bank accounts, including checking, savings, and certificates of deposit (CDs). Also, include investment accounts, such as brokerage accounts, retirement accounts (e.g., 401(k), IRA), and college savings plans (e.g., 529 plan).
   - Stocks, Bonds, and Mutual Funds: Note any individual stocks, bonds, or mutual funds you own.
   - Vehicles: Include cars, motorcycles, boats, or any other vehicles you own.
   - Personal Property: List valuable personal items like jewelry, artwork, antiques, electronics, or other collectibles.
   - Business Interests: If you own a business or have shares in a company, include those assets.
   - Life Insurance: Note any life insurance policies you have, including their cash value.
   - Other Assets: This category can include anything of value not mentioned above, such as patents, copyrights, royalties, or intellectual property.

2. Debts:
   - Mortgage: Include the outstanding balance on your mortgage or any other property loans.
   - Loans: Note any outstanding personal loans, student loans, or auto loans.
   - Credit Card Balances: List the balances on your credit cards.
   - Other Debts: This category can include any other outstanding debts, such as medical bills or personal lines of credit.

It's important to be thorough and accurate when listing your assets and debts. Keep supporting documents, such as account statements, loan agreements, or property deeds, organized and easily accessible.

Regularly review and update your asset and debt list as your financial situation changes. This could include acquiring new assets, paying off debts, or making significant financial decisions.

Having a clear understanding of your assets and debts can help with financial planning, budgeting, and making informed decisions about your estate, investments, or retirement plans. If you're unsure or need assistance, consider consulting with a financial advisor or estate planning professional who can guide you through the process.

D. Designating Guardians for Minor Children

Designating guardians for minor children is an important step in ensuring their well-being and care in the event that something happens to you as a parent or legal guardian. Here are some guidelines to help you through the process:

1. Consider your values and preferences: Think about what values and beliefs are important to you and how you would like your children to be raised. Consider factors such as religious or cultural beliefs, educational values, discipline methods, and lifestyle choices.

2. Identify potential guardians: Make a list of potential guardians who you trust and believe would provide a loving and supportive environment for your children. This can include family members, close friends, or other individuals who have a strong bond with your children.

3. Have open and honest conversations: Talk to the potential guardians about your intentions and ensure they are willing and able to take on the responsibility. Discuss your expectations, values, and any specific concerns you may have. It's important to choose someone who is willing and capable of providing the care and support your children need.

4. Consider practical factors: Take into account practical factors such as the potential guardian's age, health, financial stability, and current family situation. Assess whether they have the ability to provide for your children's physical, emotional, and financial needs.

5. Create legal documentation: Consult with an attorney to create a legally binding document, such as a will or a standalone guardianship designation, that clearly states your chosen guardian(s) for your minor children. Make sure to include any specific instructions or wishes you have regarding your children's upbringing.

6. Review and update regularly: Periodically review your choice of guardians to ensure they are still the best fit for your children's needs. Circumstances can change over time, so it's important to keep your guardianship designation up to date.

7. Communicate your decision: Inform your chosen guardians about your decision and provide them with copies of the legal documentation. It may also be helpful to communicate your wishes to other family members or close friends who may be involved in your children's lives.

Remember, designating guardians for your minor children is a personal decision. It's important to choose someone who shares your values and whom you trust to provide a loving and nurturing environment for your children. Seeking professional advice from an attorney can help ensure that your wishes are properly documented and legally binding.

VI. Estate Planning Considerations

A. Understanding Probate

Probate is a legal process that takes place after someone passes away. It involves the court overseeing the distribution of the deceased person's assets and settling their debts. Here are some key points to help you understand probate:

1. Purpose of Probate: The primary purpose of probate is to ensure that the deceased person's assets are distributed correctly and in

accordance with their wishes or applicable laws. It provides a legal framework for the orderly transfer of property and resolves any outstanding financial obligations.

2. Executor/Administrator: The probate process is typically initiated by the executor or administrator of the deceased person's estate. This person is responsible for managing the estate, including identifying and valuing assets, paying debts and taxes, and distributing the remaining assets to beneficiaries.

3. Will and Intestate Succession: If the deceased person left a valid will, it will guide the distribution of their assets. The court will review the will to ensure its validity and appoint the executor named in the will. If there is no will or the will is deemed invalid, the court will follow intestate succession laws to determine how the assets will be distributed.

4. Probate Court Involvement: The probate court oversees the probate process to ensure that it is conducted fairly and in accordance with the law. The court may require the executor to file various documents, such as an inventory of assets, and may also hold hearings to address any disputes or issues that arise during the probate process.

5. Creditors and Debt Settlement: During probate, the deceased person's debts, including outstanding loans, taxes, and funeral expenses, are typically settled using the assets of the estate. Creditors are given the opportunity to make claims against the estate, and the executor will pay these debts from the available assets.

6. Distribution of Assets: Once all debts and expenses have been settled, the remaining assets are distributed to the beneficiaries as outlined in the will or determined by intestate succession laws. This distribution is supervised by the court to ensure fairness and compliance with the deceased person's wishes or applicable laws.

7. Length and Cost of Probate: The length and cost of probate can vary depending on factors such as the complexity of the estate, the number of creditors, and any disputes that may arise. Probate can

sometimes be a lengthy process, taking several months or even years to complete. Additionally, there may be court fees and legal expenses associated with probate.

It's important to note that probate laws and processes may vary by jurisdiction, so it's advisable to seek legal advice from an attorney familiar with the laws in your area if you have specific questions or concerns about probate.

B. Minimizing Estate Taxes

Minimizing estate taxes is a common goal for many individuals who want to pass on their assets to their loved ones while minimizing the tax burden. Here are some strategies that can be used to help reduce estate taxes:

1. Estate Planning: Proper estate planning is essential to minimize estate taxes. Working with an experienced estate planning attorney can help ensure that your assets are structured in a way that maximizes tax efficiency. This may involve setting up trusts, creating a gifting strategy, or utilizing other estate planning tools.

2. Lifetime Gifting: Making gifts during your lifetime can help reduce the size of your taxable estate. The annual gift tax exclusion allows you to gift a certain amount of money or assets to individuals each year without incurring any gift tax. By gifting assets over time, you can gradually decrease the value of your estate subject to taxation.

3. Irrevocable Life Insurance Trust (ILIT): An ILIT is a trust that owns a life insurance policy on your life. By transferring the policy to an ILIT, the proceeds can be kept outside of your taxable estate. This can be an effective way to provide for your loved ones while minimizing estate taxes.

4. Charitable Giving: Donating to qualified charities or establishing a charitable trust can provide both philanthropic benefits and tax

advantages. Charitable contributions are generally deductible from your taxable estate, reducing the overall tax liability.

5. Family Limited Partnership (FLP) or Limited Liability Company (LLC): Creating an FLP or LLC allows you to transfer assets to the partnership or company and then gift or sell shares to family members. This can help reduce the value of your taxable estate while still allowing you to maintain control over the assets.

6. Qualified Personal Residence Trust (QPRT): A QPRT allows you to transfer your primary residence or vacation home to an irrevocable trust while retaining the right to use the property for a specified period. This can help reduce the value of your taxable estate while still allowing you to live in the property.

7. Estate Tax Exemption and Portability: Understanding the estate tax exemption limit and portability rules is crucial. The exemption is the amount of assets that can pass tax-free at the time of your death. Portability allows a surviving spouse to utilize any unused portion of the deceased spouse's exemption. By maximizing the use of exemptions and portability, you can minimize estate taxes.

It's important to note that estate tax laws can be complex and may vary by jurisdiction. Consulting with a qualified estate planning attorney or tax professional is recommended to develop a tailored strategy that aligns with your specific circumstances and goals.

C. Establishing Trusts

Establishing trusts is a common estate planning strategy that can provide various benefits and help achieve specific goals. A trust is a legal entity that holds assets on behalf of beneficiaries, and it is managed by a trustee. Here are some types of trusts and their purposes:

1. Revocable Living Trust: Also known as a living trust or inter vivos trust, this trust is created during your lifetime and can be modified or revoked as long as you are still alive and mentally competent. The primary purpose of a revocable living trust is to avoid probate, which is the legal process of administering a deceased

person's estate. By placing assets into the trust, they can pass directly to beneficiaries without going through probate, which can save time and costs.

2. Irrevocable Trust: Unlike a revocable trust, an irrevocable trust cannot be changed or revoked once it is established. This type of trust is often used for asset protection, tax planning, and Medicaid planning. By transferring assets into an irrevocable trust, you remove them from your taxable estate, potentially reducing estate taxes. Additionally, the assets in an irrevocable trust may be protected from creditors and lawsuits, providing a level of asset protection.

3. Testamentary Trust: A testamentary trust is created through a person's will and only takes effect upon their death. This type of trust allows you to specify how your assets should be managed and distributed after your passing. Testamentary trusts are commonly used when there are minor or disabled beneficiaries who may not be capable of managing their inheritance.

4. Special Needs Trust: A special needs trust is designed to provide for the needs of a disabled individual without jeopardizing their eligibility for government benefits. By placing assets in a special needs trust, the funds can be used to supplement the beneficiary's needs beyond what government assistance provides, while still allowing them to qualify for benefits like Medicaid or Supplemental Security Income (SSI).

5. Charitable Trust: A charitable trust allows you to make a charitable contribution while still receiving some financial benefits. There are two main types of charitable trusts: charitable remainder trusts and charitable lead trusts. A charitable remainder trust provides income to the donor or other beneficiaries for a specified period, with the remainder going to a charitable organization. A charitable lead trust, on the other hand, provides income to a charitable organization for a specified period, with the remainder going to non-charitable beneficiaries.

6. Dynasty Trust: A dynasty trust is designed to provide for multiple generations of beneficiaries, potentially avoiding estate taxes for

future generations. By placing assets in a dynasty trust, they can be protected from estate taxes and creditors, allowing the wealth to grow and benefit future family members.

These are just a few examples of the types of trusts that can be established. The specific trust or combination of trusts that are appropriate for you will depend on your goals, financial situation, and the laws of your jurisdiction. Consulting with an experienced estate planning attorney or financial advisor is recommended to determine the best trust structure for your needs.

VII. Updating and Revoking Your Will

A. Reasons for Updating

There are several reasons why it is important to regularly update your estate plan and make changes as needed. Here are some key reasons:

1. Changes in Family Circumstances: Over time, your family circumstances may change. This can include births, deaths, marriages, divorces, or other significant events. Updating your estate plan ensures that your assets are distributed according to your current wishes and that your designated beneficiaries and heirs are up-to-date.

2. Changes in Financial Situation: Your financial situation may evolve over time. This can include changes in income, investments, property ownership, or business interests. Updating your estate plan allows you to account for these changes and ensure that your assets are properly managed and distributed to align with your financial goals.

3. Changes in Tax Laws: Tax laws are subject to frequent changes, and these changes can impact your estate plan. By staying informed about any updates to tax laws, you can make necessary adjustments to your plan to minimize tax liabilities and maximize the benefits for your beneficiaries.

4. Changes in Personal Goals: Your personal goals and priorities may shift over time. You may have new philanthropic endeavors, charitable interests, or specific wishes for the distribution of your assets. Regularly reviewing and updating your estate plan allows you to align your plan with your current values and goals.

5. Changes in Asset Ownership: If you acquire or dispose of significant assets, such as real estate, businesses, or investments, it is important to update your estate plan accordingly. This ensures that these assets are properly included or excluded from your plan and that the appropriate strategies are in place to protect and distribute them.

6. Changes in Laws and Regulations: In addition to tax laws, other laws and regulations related to estate planning, probate, and asset protection may change over time. Staying informed about these changes and updating your estate plan accordingly can help ensure that your plan remains compliant with current legal requirements and provides the intended benefits.

7. Changes in Health or Capacity: If you experience changes in your health or capacity, it is important to update your estate plan to ensure that your wishes for healthcare decisions, medical directives, and the appointment of guardians or conservators are accurately reflected.

Regularly reviewing and updating your estate plan is essential to ensure that it continues to meet your goals and objectives. Consulting with an experienced estate planning attorney or financial advisor can provide guidance on when and how to make necessary updates to your plan.

B. Proper Procedures
When it comes to updating your estate plan, it is important to follow proper procedures to ensure that the changes you make are legally valid and effective. Here are the general steps to consider:

1. Review your current estate plan: Start by reviewing your existing estate plan documents, including your will, trust, power of attorney,

healthcare directives, and any other relevant documents. Take note of any provisions or instructions that need to be updated or modified.

2. Identify the changes needed: Determine what specific changes you want to make to your estate plan. This could include updating beneficiaries, appointing new trustees or executors, changing distribution percentages, adding or removing assets, or making adjustments based on changes in tax laws or personal circumstances.

3. Seek professional advice: It is highly recommended to consult with an experienced estate planning attorney or financial advisor. They can provide guidance on the legal and financial implications of your desired changes and help you navigate the complex estate planning process.

4. Draft new documents or amend existing ones: Depending on the nature of the changes, you may need to either draft new estate planning documents or amend existing ones. For simple changes, such as updating beneficiary designations, a separate document called a codicil or amendment may be sufficient. For more significant changes, a complete redrafting of the documents may be necessary.

5. Execute the updated documents: Once the new documents or amendments have been prepared, you will need to sign them in the presence of witnesses and a notary public, as required by law. This ensures that the changes are legally valid and enforceable.

6. Communicate the changes: It is important to communicate the updated estate plan to your loved ones, beneficiaries, trustees, and anyone else who needs to be aware of the changes. This helps avoid confusion or disputes in the future and ensures that everyone understands your intentions.

7. Update beneficiary designations: In addition to updating your estate planning documents, it is important to review and update beneficiary designations on accounts such as life insurance policies, retirement plans, and bank accounts. These designations typically

override any provisions in your will or trust, so it is crucial to keep them up to date.

8. Store and maintain the updated documents: Safely store your updated estate planning documents in a secure location and inform your trusted family members or advisors about their whereabouts. You may also consider providing copies to your appointed trustees or executors.

Remember that estate planning is an ongoing process, and it is recommended to review and update your plan every few years or whenever significant life events occur. Regularly consulting with professionals and staying informed about changes in laws and regulations will help ensure that your estate plan remains current and reflects your wishes.

VIII. DIY vs. Seeking Legal Assistance

A. Pros and Cons of DIY Will Kits

Using a do-it-yourself (DIY) will kit can be an affordable and convenient option for creating a basic will. However, it is essential to consider the pros and cons before deciding whether a DIY will kit is the right choice for you. Here are some pros and cons to consider:

Pros of DIY Will Kits:

1. Cost-effective: DIY will kits are generally more affordable than hiring an attorney to draft a will. This can be beneficial if you have a straightforward estate and limited assets.

2. Convenience: DIY will kits are readily available online or in stores, making them easily accessible. You can complete the process at your own pace and in the comfort of your own home.

3. Privacy: Some individuals prefer to keep their personal and financial matters private. Using a DIY will kit allows you to maintain confidentiality since you do not have to consult with an attorney or involve any third parties.

Cons of DIY Will Kits:

1. Complexity: Estate planning can be complex, and a DIY will kit may not adequately address all of your specific needs and circumstances. DIY kits often provide generic templates that may not account for unique family situations, tax considerations, or complex asset distributions.

2. Legal expertise: DIY will kits do not provide the same level of legal expertise and guidance as an attorney. Estate planning attorneys have in-depth knowledge of state laws and can provide personalized advice to ensure your will is legally valid and enforceable.

3. Errors and omissions: Without professional guidance, there is a higher risk of making errors or omissions in your will. These mistakes can lead to unintended consequences, disputes, or even render the will invalid.

4. Limited support: DIY will kits typically do not offer ongoing support or assistance. If you have questions or need clarification during the process, you may not have access to professional guidance.

5. Updates and changes: DIY will kits may not provide an easy way to update or make changes to your will in the future. Estate planning needs can change over time, and it is important to have a flexible and adaptable document.

6. Potential challenges: DIY wills may be more susceptible to legal challenges or disputes due to potential errors, unclear language, or lack of professional oversight.

It is important to note that the effectiveness of a DIY will kit may vary depending on individual circumstances. If your estate is complex, you have significant assets, or you have specific concerns or objectives, consulting with an experienced estate planning attorney is strongly recommended. An attorney can provide personalized advice, ensure your wishes are properly documented, and help minimize potential risks and complications.

C. Benefits of Consulting an Attorney

Consulting an attorney for legal matters, such as creating a will, can provide numerous benefits. Here are some of the key advantages of seeking professional advice from an attorney:

1. Legal Expertise: Attorneys have comprehensive knowledge of the law and can provide expert guidance tailored to your specific situation. They stay updated on changes in legislation and understand the complexities of estate planning, ensuring that your will is drafted accurately and in compliance with relevant laws.

2. Personalized Advice: Every individual's circumstances are unique, and an attorney can provide personalized advice based on your specific needs and goals. They can help you navigate complex family dynamics, tax considerations, and asset distribution to ensure your wishes are properly documented and legally enforceable.

3. Customization: An attorney can help you create a will that reflects your exact wishes and preferences. They can assist in drafting provisions that address specific concerns, such as guardianship for minor children, charitable bequests, or special instructions for the distribution of assets.

4. Avoiding Mistakes and Omissions: Estate planning involves intricate legal requirements, and DIY approaches may lead to errors or omissions that can have serious consequences. Attorneys have the expertise to identify potential issues and ensure that your will is accurate, comprehensive, and free from common mistakes.

5. Minimizing Disputes and Challenges: A well-drafted will can help minimize the risk of disputes among family members or other potential beneficiaries. Attorneys can provide guidance on how to structure your will to reduce the likelihood of legal challenges and ensure that your intentions are clear and legally binding.

6. Tax Planning: Attorneys experienced in estate planning can assist you in implementing strategies to minimize estate taxes and maximize the value of your assets for your beneficiaries. They can

help you understand the potential tax implications of different decisions and explore options to optimize your estate plan.

7. Ongoing Support: Consulting an attorney provides ongoing support beyond just the creation of a will. They can assist with updating your will as your circumstances change, answer any legal questions or concerns that arise, and provide guidance on other related matters, such as trusts, powers of attorney, and healthcare directives.

8. Peace of Mind: Knowing that your estate plan has been professionally and meticulously prepared can provide peace of mind. Consulting an attorney ensures that your wishes will be carried out according to your intentions, and that your loved ones will be protected and provided for.

While consulting an attorney may involve an upfront cost, the long-term benefits and security that come with professional legal advice often outweigh the potential risks and complications that may arise from a DIY approach.

IX. Common Questions and Concerns

A. What happens if I die without a will?

If you die without a will, your estate will be distributed according to the laws of intestacy in your jurisdiction. Here are some common outcomes that can occur if you pass away without a will:

1. State Laws Determine Distribution: The laws of intestacy vary from one jurisdiction to another, but generally, they dictate how your assets will be distributed among your surviving family members. Typically, your spouse and children are given priority, followed by other relatives if you have no immediate family.

2. Potential Disputes and Delays: Without a will, there is a higher likelihood of disputes among family members regarding the distribution of assets. This can lead to delays in the probate process and can strain relationships between loved ones.

3. Lack of Control: Dying without a will means you have no say in how your assets will be distributed. Your estate will be divided according to the default laws, which may not align with your preferences. This can result in unintended beneficiaries receiving assets or loved ones being left out.

4. Guardianship Determination: If you have minor children, dying without a will means that the court will decide who will be their guardian. This decision may not align with your wishes or what you believe is in the best interest of your children.

5. Increased Costs: The probate process without a will can be more complex and time-consuming, resulting in higher legal fees and court costs. The lack of clear instructions can also lead to additional expenses, such as hiring experts to locate potential heirs or resolve disputes.

6. Potential Loss of Assets: In some cases, if no eligible heirs are found, or if the estate remains unclaimed, your assets may escheat to the state. This means that the government becomes the legal owner of your property.

7. Lack of Charitable Contributions: If you have philanthropic intentions and wish to leave assets to charitable organizations, dying without a will means those intentions may not be realized. Without clear instructions, your assets may not go to the causes you care about.

To avoid these potential consequences, it is advisable to consult with an attorney to create a valid will that reflects your wishes. A will provides clarity, reduces the risk of disputes, and ensures that your assets are distributed according to your intentions.

B. Can I change my will after it is created?

Yes, you can change your will after it is created. It is common for people to update their wills as their circumstances change or their wishes evolve. Here are some ways you can make changes to your will:

1. Codicil: A codicil is a legal document that amends specific provisions of an existing will while leaving the rest of the will intact. It is a useful option for making minor changes, such as updating beneficiaries or adding or removing specific assets. A codicil must meet the same legal requirements as a will and should be signed and witnessed accordingly.

2. Revocation and New Will: Another option is to revoke your existing will and create a new one. This involves drafting a new will that reflects your updated wishes and specifically revoking any previous wills. Creating a new will is recommended for more significant changes or when multiple changes need to be made.

3. Will Amendment: Some jurisdictions allow for a simpler version of a codicil known as a will amendment or will amendment form. This is a separate document that can be used to make changes to a will without having to create an entirely new will. It is important to check the laws of your jurisdiction regarding the validity and requirements of a will amendment.

Regardless of the method you choose, it is essential to ensure that any changes to your will are legally valid. It is advisable to consult with an attorney who specializes in estate planning to guide you through the process and ensure that your updated will accurately reflects your wishes. Additionally, it is important to keep your updated will in a safe and accessible place and inform your loved ones of its existence and location.

C. How often should I review and update my will?

It is generally recommended to review and update your will periodically to ensure that it accurately reflects your current wishes and circumstances. While there is no set rule for how often you should review your will, here are some situations that may prompt a review:

1. Significant life events: Any major life changes, such as marriage, divorce, the birth or adoption of a child, or the death of a beneficiary, may necessitate updates to your will. It is important to review your

will after such events to ensure that your assets are distributed according to your current wishes.

2. Changes in financial situation: If there have been significant changes in your financial situation, such as acquiring new assets, selling property, or starting a business, it may be necessary to update your will to reflect these changes and ensure that your assets are distributed as you intend.

3. Relocation: If you have moved to a different jurisdiction, it is important to review your will to ensure that it complies with the laws of your new location. Estate planning laws can vary between jurisdictions, and updating your will can help avoid any complications in the future.

4. Changes in relationships: Changes in your relationships with beneficiaries or executors named in your will may also warrant a review. If you have had a falling out with a beneficiary or if your relationship with your chosen executor has changed, it may be necessary to update your will accordingly.

5. Changes in tax laws: Tax laws and regulations are subject to change, and these changes can have implications for your estate plan. It is advisable to review your will periodically to ensure that it remains tax-efficient and takes advantage of any available tax planning strategies.

It is a good practice to review your will at least every few years, even if there have been no significant changes in your life. This can help ensure that your will remains up to date and accurately reflects your wishes. Consulting with an attorney who specializes in estate planning can provide you with guidance and assistance in reviewing and updating your will.

X. CONCLUSION

A. Taking Control of Your Legacy

Taking control of your legacy involves actively planning and making decisions about how you want to be remembered and how your assets and possessions will be distributed after your passing. Here are some steps you can take to take control of your legacy:

1. Define your values and priorities: Start by reflecting on what is most important to you and what you want to be remembered for. Consider your personal values, beliefs, and goals. This will provide a foundation for making decisions about your legacy.

2. Create a will: A will is a legal document that outlines how you want your assets to be distributed after your death. It allows you to specify who will inherit your property, who will be the guardian of your children, and who will manage your affairs. Consult with an attorney to ensure your will is properly drafted and reflects your wishes.

3. Consider a trust: A trust is another estate planning tool that allows you to transfer your assets to a designated trustee to manage and distribute according to your instructions. Trusts can provide flexibility, privacy, and potential tax advantages. Consult with an attorney to determine if a trust is appropriate for your situation.

4. Communicate your wishes: It is important to have open and honest conversations with your loved ones about your end-of-life wishes and your plans for your legacy. This can help prevent misunderstandings and conflicts among family members and ensure that your wishes are known and respected.

5. Plan for charitable giving: If philanthropy is important to you, consider including charitable giving as part of your legacy plan. You can designate specific charities or create a charitable foundation to support causes that align with your values.

6. Consider legacy planning beyond financial assets: Your legacy is not just about money and possessions. Think about the impact you want to have on future generations. This can include passing on family traditions, values, stories, and wisdom. Consider documenting your life experiences, writing letters to your loved ones, or creating a family legacy project.

7. Review and update regularly: Life is constantly changing, so it's important to review and update your legacy plan regularly. Major life events, such as marriage, divorce, birth, or death, may require revisions to your plan. Regularly reviewing and updating your plan ensures that it remains current and aligned with your wishes.

Taking control of your legacy involves thoughtful planning, communication, and regular review. By proactively making decisions about your legacy, you can have peace of mind knowing that your wishes will be carried out and your impact will be felt even after you're gone.

B. Importance of Planning Ahead

Planning ahead is crucial in various aspects of life, as it allows you to anticipate and prepare for the future. Here are some reasons why planning ahead is important:

1. Preparedness: Planning ahead helps you be prepared for unforeseen circumstances or emergencies. By thinking ahead and considering potential challenges or risks, you can develop contingency plans and have the necessary resources in place to mitigate any potential negative impacts.

2. Goal Achievement: Planning ahead allows you to set clear goals and create a roadmap to achieve them. Whether it's personal goals, career objectives, or financial targets, having a plan in place helps you stay focused, motivated, and organized. It enables you to break down big goals into smaller, manageable steps, increasing the likelihood of success.

3. Time Management: Planning ahead helps you effectively manage your time. By mapping out your tasks, deadlines, and priorities in

advance, you can allocate your time efficiently and avoid last-minute rushes or procrastination. This ensures that you have enough time for important activities and reduces stress caused by disorganization or lack of time management.

4. Financial Stability: Planning ahead is crucial for financial stability and security. By creating a budget, saving for the future, and planning for retirement, you can ensure that you have a solid financial foundation. Planning ahead also helps you make informed decisions about investments, insurance, and estate planning, allowing you to protect and grow your wealth over time.

5. Reduced Stress: Planning ahead reduces stress and anxiety by providing a sense of control and confidence in the face of uncertainty. When you have a plan in place, you can approach challenges or changes with a proactive mindset, knowing that you have considered various scenarios and have strategies in place to deal with them.

6. Improved Decision-Making: Planning ahead gives you time to gather information, evaluate options, and make informed decisions. It allows you to weigh the pros and cons, consider different perspectives, and make choices based on careful thought rather than impulsivity. This leads to better decision-making and reduces the likelihood of regretting hasty or uninformed choices.

7. Legacy and Impact: Planning ahead allows you to shape your legacy and make a positive impact on future generations. By considering your values, goals, and aspirations, you can create a plan that aligns with your vision for the future. Whether it's through charitable giving, mentoring, or leaving a lasting impact in your professional or personal life, planning ahead enables you to leave a meaningful legacy.

In summary, planning ahead is essential for preparedness, goal achievement, time management, financial stability, stress reduction, improved decision-making, and creating a lasting impact. By taking the time to plan and prepare, you can navigate life with greater confidence, purpose, and success.

Dear Readers,

Thank you so much for your purchase! I truly appreciate your support and hope that the book brings you valuable insights and inspiration.

Your feedback is incredibly important to me. If you have a few moments to spare, I kindly ask you to leave an honest review of the book. Your review will not only help me understand how I can improve, but it will also guide potential readers in making informed decisions.

I value your opinion and would love to hear about your experience with the book. Your feedback will assist me in creating more meaningful content and serving my readers better.

Once again, thank you for your purchase and for considering leaving a review. I'm grateful for your support and hope to continue providing you with valuable resources in the future.

Mark Livingston

www.ingramcontent.com/pod-product-compliance
Lightning Source LLC
Chambersburg PA
CBHW070955220526
45471CB00007B/3039